GUESS THAT ANIMAL!

NAME THE AMPHIBIAN!

By Demi Jackson

Gareth Stevens
PUBLISHING

Please visit our website, www.garethstevens.com. For a free color catalog of all our high-quality books, call toll free 1-800-542-2595 or fax 1-877-542-2596.

Library of Congress Cataloging-in-Publication Data

Names: Jackson, Demi, author.
Title: Name that amphibian! / Demi Jackson.
Description: New York : Gareth Stevens Publishing, [2017] | Series: Guess
  that animal! | Includes bibliographical references and index.
Identifiers: LCCN 2015045641 | ISBN 9781482447484 (pbk.) | ISBN 9781482447415
(library bound) | ISBN 9781482446982 (6 pack)
Subjects: LCSH: Amphibians–Juvenile literature.
Classification: LCC QL644.2 .J33 2017 | DDC 597.8–dc23
LC record available at http://lccn.loc.gov/2015045641

Published in 2017 by
Gareth Stevens Publishing
111 East 14th Street, Suite 349
New York, NY 10003

Designer: Andrea Davison-Bartolotta
Editor: Kristen Nelson

Photo credits: Cover, p. 1 mark tipping/Shutterstock.com; p. 5 Javier Fernández
Sánchez/Moment Open/Getty Images; pp. 7, 9 London Scientific Films/Oxford
Scientific/Getty Images; pp. 11, 13 Ondrej Prosicky/Shutterstock.com; pp. 15, 17
Peter Reijners/Shutterstock.com; pp. 19, 21 belizar/Shutterstock.com.

Printed in the United States of America

CPSIA compliance information: Batch #CS16GS: For further information contact Gareth Stevens, New York, New York at 1-800-542-2595.

CONTENTS

Boldface words appear in the glossary.

Get to Know Amphibians

Toads, frogs, salamanders, newts, and caecilians (sih-SIHL-yuhnz) are all amphibians! The word "amphibian" comes from a word that means "double life." They spend part of their life in water and part on land. Let's see some of these cool **creatures** up close!

What's on the Cover?

It's a newt! Newts are kinds of salamanders, which are amphibians that have tails when they're fully grown.

Growing Up

Could you swim without your arms or legs? This baby amphibian does! It has a small, round body and a wide tail. It moves through the water and eats tiny plants. What is it?

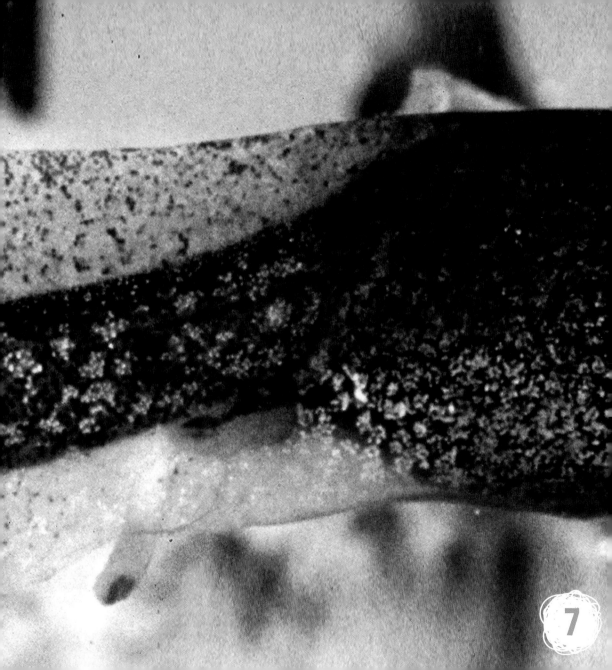

It's a tadpole! Tadpoles are the larvae of frogs and toads that **hatch** from eggs. Frogs and toads may stay tadpoles for a few weeks or a few years! Tadpoles grow legs and lose their tail as they grow into adults.

Spot Some Spots

Bright yellow or orange spots should be easy to see, right? Nope! This amphibian likes to live in dark, wet places. Its bright spots send a message to **predators**. It produces a **toxin** that tastes bad! What amphibian has skin like this?

It's the spotted salamander! Like other amphibians, salamanders start life in an egg. Then, larvae grow in the water before changing into adults. Adult spotted salamanders live in forests and only come out of hiding to eat at night!

Twinkle Toes

Every kind of this amphibian has special feet! The bone of their last toe is shaped like a claw. Their toes have sticky pads on them to help them climb. Which amphibian has feet like this?

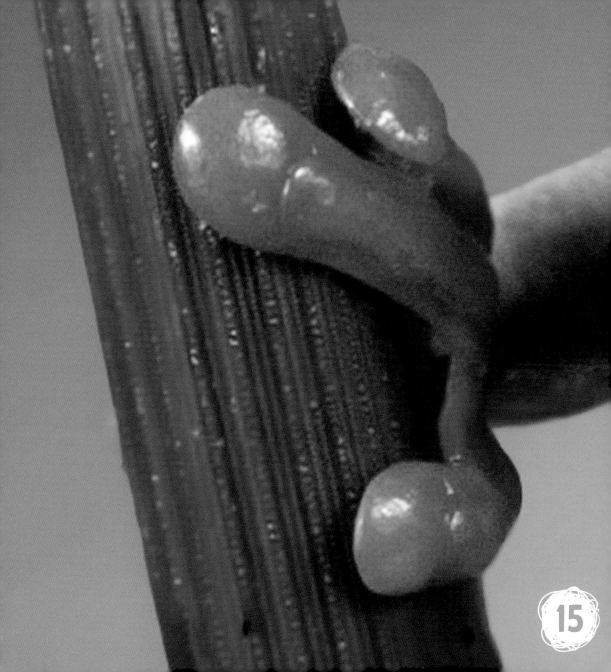

It's a tree frog! There are more than 800 species, or kinds, of tree frogs. Not all of them live in trees, but those that do are commonly small. Like many other frogs, tree frogs eat ants, flies, and other bugs.

Warty

Most amphibians have wet-looking skin, but this bumpy, green-brown skin looks dry. Don't touch it, though. This amphibian makes toxins in **glands** behind its big eyes to keep predators away. What kind of amphibian has skin like this?

19

This warty amphibian is a common toad! These toads only live in water when they lay eggs. The rest of the year, the common toad likes to live in leaf piles and holes in the ground. People often see them in the garden!

GLOSSARY

creature: a living thing

gland: a body part that produces something needed for a bodily function

hatch: to break open or come out of

predator: an animal that hunts other animals for food

toxin: a kind of poison

FOR MORE INFORMATION

BOOKS

Hall, Katharine. *Amphibians and Reptiles: A Compare and Contrast Book*. Mt. Pleasant, SC: Arbordale Publishing, 2015.

Lewis, Clare. *Amphibian Body Parts*. Chicago, IL: Heinemann Raintree, 2016.

Schuh, Mari C. *The World's Biggest Amphibians*. Minneapolis, MN: Jump!, Inc., 2016.

WEBSITES

Amphibians
kids.sandiegozoo.org/animals/amphibians
Find out much more about amphibians, and use links to learn about other kinds of animals, too.

Amphibians
www.neok12.com/Amphibians.htm
Take quizzes about amphibians, and watch videos of an African bullfrog, a poison dart frog, and more.

INDEX